I0528725

# DREAMS
## OF A
## LANDSCAPE

# DREAMS
# OF A
# LANDSCAPE

a poetry chapbook

Michael Orlando Mancarella

ISBN 979-8-9918797-5-0


Cover Art & Design: John Mancarella

Editor: Emily Price Soli


Some poems were first published (in slightly different form) to michaelorlandopoetry.com and by email as part of *Bird Sounds & Sunlight*.

to J.R. & R.R.

# CONTENTS

The terrain,
autumn 2021 to spring 2022.

## PAINTED

The trees have some tinges
of reds, oranges, and yellows,
yet the insects still creak
into the night air,
and today still held
one or two
morning glory blossoms.
Maybe early fall
still carries some summer
in her stride,
but gradually she will
put these elements down
and the world around me
will continue to transform.
And where will I be
in my own seasons?
Will I change innerly
in ways I wish?
And will my self-expression
be like the tones
to be painted across the landscape?

## RAIN & SUN

With the rain still heavy,
out the fourth-floor window
of the medical complex's common area
was a spindly spider dangling,
rappelling headfirst down the pane.

I felt something about his need
to survive, but even if I could've
let him in those windows that don't open,
he'd not likely do well inside.
He has to be out there
and be resilient.

So I meandered,
then returned
to where the spider had been,
and in a corner
was a small cross placed
on a note saying one
was welcome
to take it.

That evening we were all held
in the copper light
of a dipping sun filtered through clouds
shining on everything wet
like it had rained all day.

# A FINE AUTUMN DAY

I took a walk in the neighborhood—
it was sunny and comfortable.
The various leaves on the sidewalk
were wet from yesterday's storm.
I walked farther than usual,
and on my way home, I saw a man
sauntering along and playing a ukulele.
Drawing near, he gave me an open look.
"How are you, my friend?
Beautiful day."
I said, "Good day for a uke!"
"Yes, sir!" he said,
and he continued on,
creating a world around him—
and I listened to the strumming
as it faded into the distance
until I couldn't tell
if I were hearing
or remembering
the sound of a ukulele
on a fine autumn day.

## SOMEPLACE NEW

Certain terrains of the psyche
are recognizable to me:
bogs of depression,
crags of anxiety,
and languishing's parched ground.

Today, what was that field inside me
that opened up?

I think it was
joy of purpose.

GIFTS

Going out to my car,
the air is relaxed for
a November evening.

Running late, and
still enough time
to gaze at the moon.

## SENSIBILITY

The break in clouds on this silvery day
showing a swath of blue—

The aqua pool of water
resting on kindly snow—

The bundled layers wrapping me
in winter's sensibility—

I feel their tender beauty.

## TO UNCOVER

It's this
biting wind that moved
the clouds
to uncover
the sun.

## A LITTLE JOY

For stretches of my life,
anxiety kept me
from looking forward to things.
And now, here, something little:
I just anticipated walking through a piece of sunlight.

# A MAN REMINDED ME

In the egg aisle, a man reminded me
of my American-born Italian grandpa.
His hair was stark white,
growing mostly on the sides
of his bronzed head.
My gaze lingered.

After, as I pushed my cart
toward the checkout lines,
I noticed him again,
moving away from me.
Even his gait was like Grandpa's:
square, with a slight limp.

I paused, taking in this glimpse
of someone gone
long ago.

## FROM A JOURNAL ENTRY

be gentle with the not-known

## A DECEMBER DAY ABOVE FREEZING

A bug is flying
around the balcony,
and I'm thinking about
how I judge others
for the faults
that reflect my own—

Working on self-acceptance.

TOWARD

As colorless
as this overcast
day is,
if I dove up
into the clouds
far enough
and long enough,
eventually I
would come out into
sunlight.

# HOPE IN THIS FRIGID LAND

If you dreamed
this unfamiliar landscape,
what would you make of it?

The outer:
cold air,
spindly branches,
ice hanging from eaves,
crusty snow
covering the ground.

The inner:
a wound of knowing
your heart to be a book
that is hidden,
leaving you unable
to read from its pages.

Then,
a deeper memory
flutters up.
From farther back in your mind
you glimpse the environment transformed:
birds chirping,
humans clothed lightly,
lush plants blooming.
Somehow you sense a time of expansion—
you remember summer.

# THE WATERS

The noise of the dishwasher washing.
Across the apartment in an armchair,
I start listening more closely
to the cycling. There is
not just a single swipe
at the food residue—instead,
water churning repeatedly
as the dishes are cleaned.
Is this how we too change?
No one perfect action—instead,
little decisions . . .
to clasp hands,
to say no to the things of addiction,
to send a random gift,
to meditate,
to invite for dinner,
to pray . . .
and to do these things
over and over—
and in so doing,
to enter the rhythm
of a good life.

## AMBLING

walking under a pine tree
the falling snow
                    pauses

## UPON READING TRANSLATED
## CHINESE POEMS

It's getting late, but I
don't want to go to sleep.
I'm excited about plans
and potential. I'm not
tipsy like Lu Yu, but still
I can go out on the balcony
and breathe in some brisk air.
Maybe I'll find some stars.

## SPECKS

The bare woods
gilded with evening sun
stand before
a plum sky.
And then, revealed—
the first buds of spring.

# BECOMING

The grass is beginning
to stretch into richness
after its winter sleep,
and the grounds of the apartments
look dapper with new mulch
snug up to the bases of bushes
like blankets.

The struggle to learn
how to relate
to the architecture of yourself
with affection
and be true
to the form you take . . .
is it wholly human?

Pushing leaf buds into being
in the space
where vegetation
will hang at the doorstep of the sky,
the trees
flourish into their own joy.

## WHAT IS HERE

*Some ask,*
*what is there without love?*

I help with the dishes.
I wash pots and pans.
Being around others,
I feel fullness and purpose:
a chilly psyche
now wrapped
in a cozy robe.

*Some ask,*
*what is there without love?*
*I'd say,*
*the journey to love.*

## TREES AT NIGHT

Trees sometimes—
and I think this while seeing them
partly illumined by building lights
from below—
seem like mythical creatures.
So patient, so slow, so kind,
they watch over us
while stretching toward the sky.
Maybe, though we might not realize it,
this is what we need.

SPRING

A brook
weaves through the woodland
in late afternoon sun.
Leafy plants
have appeared
near its banks
like green napkins
folded and placed
in preparation for a celebration.
Perhaps birds will arrive,
insects, squirrels, spiders,
chipmunks, maybe even a deer . . .
I imagine it all
as I pause on my walk,
captivated for a moment
by a shimmering brook.

## FOR SOMEONE WHO HAS LANGUISHED

maybe
the universe
we live in
is not like
I thought
it was

such
good
news

## ABOUT THE AUTHOR

Michael Orlando Mancarella is a poet living in southern New Hampshire. After his schooling on the East Coast, he settled in California for a few years before returning to his home state. Through his writing project, *Bird Sounds & Sunlight*, he sends poetry to readers by email.

## ABOUT THE TYPE

This book's text is set in EB Garamond, an open-source typeface released by Georg Duffner in 2011. It was created from the Egenolff-Berner specimen of 1592, which shows the work of Claude Garamont and Robert Granjon, who, respectively, designed the original Garamond typeface and its matching italic characters.

www.ingramcontent.com/pod-product-compliance
Lightning Source LLC
Chambersburg PA
CBHW020922140626
46545CB00015B/1221